A CURMUDGEON'S GUIDE TO POSTMODERN TIMES

 A catalogue record for this book is available from the National Library of Australia

© Richard Greene

Published 2021
Revised 2022

ISBN: 978-0-6454300-4-2 (epub)
ISBN: 978-0-6454300-3-5 (paperback)
ISBN: 978-0-6454300-5-9 (PDF)

Published with the aid of Jumble Books and Publishers (jumblebooksandpublishers.com).

Richard Greene is a poet, or has been at least since he retired from a 38-year career in international development. A lawyer by training, he fell into his development career by accident when, after law school, though planning not to practice law but interested in international affairs, he accepted an unsolicited job offer from the U.S. Agency for International Development. After a few years in Washington (or Foggy Bottom, as the location of the U.S. foreign policy establishment is known), he was assigned as legal advisor to the USAID mission in Laos and there discovered that the development business suited his interests and inclinations very well.

Greene wrote poetry beginning in the 8th grade and continued through college where he studied with a Professor, Henry Rago, who later became editor of *Poetry* magazine, the leading U.S. poetry journal. However, he wrote few poems after law school as he became absorbed in international development, but turned back to poetry as he neared retirement.

One day he noticed that a couple of the lines in one of his poems stood well on their own. He thinks the lines may have been 'The cannon is callous / in its choice of targets'. After he came up with that first aphorism, he began looking for other extractable scraps of wisdom in his poems and soon thereafter began writing such scraps independently.

This image is in the public domain.

Image Credit: Le nouvel Atlas (The New Atlas) by Honoré Daumier.

A Curmudgeon's Guide to Postmodern Times

Aphorisms

by

Richard Greene

aphorism (noun)

1: a concise statement of a principle.
2: a terse formulation of a truth or sentiment: ADAGE // the high-minded *aphorism*, 'Let us value the quality of life, not the quantity'.
3: an ingeniously terse style of expression: aphoristic language // These are dazzling chapters, packed with perfectly chosen anecdotes and pithy with *aphorism*—John Keegan.

(From: Merriam-Webster.com)

Contents

Human Nature 1
Philosophy 16
Profundity 17
Politics 19
Economics 32
Justice 35
Religion 38
Folly 51
Fashion 52
Materialism 54
The Arts 57
Poetry 64
Advice 73
Etcetera 76

Human Nature

Only unfulfilled love is perfect. All other kinds require tolerance for human defects.

Sex wouldn't be nearly so interesting if it weren't so widely forbidden.

What's sauce for the goose isn't necessarily sauce for the gander.

Some use their intellect to seek truth, others to justify their preconceptions.

The truly strong are those who aren't driven by the need to prove their strength.

Lawyers, actors and politicians must fool others. In the process they often fool themselves.

We tend to forget that not all mothers are saints, nor all soldiers heroes.

All mothers are virgins in their children's eyes.

Bird watching and yoga have become competitive sports. What does that tell you about our society?

We live in a society in which actors are seen as more important than those they portray.

Nobody climbs Everest because it's there. They climb it because that's where the top of the pecking order is.

The problem with people who are cool is that they often lack warmth.

Man is unique among animals. It's the only one with a sense of self-importance.

When the team we root for wins, we think ourselves superior.

Mankind is an endangering species.

We hate and fear rejection because it makes us feel we were stupid to ask.

We are all part miscreant, part hero.

Don't confuse writers with the values they espouse; just because they applaud virtue doesn't mean they practice it.

Speed limits were made to be exceeded.

Ponce de Leon was looking in the wrong place. While he searched Florida for the fountain of youth, he was carrying it in his head all along.

As parents we tend to overcompensate for the shortcomings of our own upbringings.

Sometimes we achieve peace more through struggle than detachment, provided the struggle is not on one's own behalf, but for the benefit of others.

Cynics are as often disillusioned idealists as callous egoists.

There are as many centers of the universe as there are people.

Man is an animal with grandiose ideas.

Flattery will get you almost anywhere.

We have mastered time and are its slaves.

We are joined to our children by constricting bands of empathy.

Human beings are the opposite of butterflies. We turn into caterpillars.

Sometimes the greatest sophisticates are the greatest naïfs.

Let's not forget that great men aren't always good men.

The Holocaust, the Khmer Rouge, Ruanda, Darfur. What kind of animal is man?

Some people are sheep in wolves' clothing.

We see others' irrationality, but not out own.

One doesn't have to get angry because somebody else does.

Humans have great difficulty accepting themselves for what they are.

If you can imagine it, somebody's done it, and, if you can't imagine it, somebody's done that too.

The human animal is much preoccupied with reproduction.

We have the notion that it's somehow noble to be human. It's true that we have exceptional capabilities compared to other members of the animal kingdom, but among those capabilities are an exceptional aptitude for doing harm to, even destroying, other creatures, our own kind, and our planet.

Intellectualizing is what intellectuals accuse each other of doing.

We accumulate things to do like barnacles.

The main challenge to human welfare is human nature.

The trouble with Freud was that he suffered from uterus envy.

It's too bad we don't suffer from *pre*-traumatic stress syndrome. There might be fewer wars.

We're intelligent enough to imperil our planet. Let's hope we're intelligent enough to save it from ourselves.

Words are the source of most human strife.

We get along so well with dogs because they can't talk back.

Even saints aren't altogether saintly.

When someone undermines our dignity we want to inflict the same pain on them, to restore the balance.

We devote so much effort to perfecting the quality of our lives that it ends up detracting from their quality.

Sometimes the fool is wiser than the wise men.

Personal libraries are a form of ostentation.

Now I know what over the hill means. It's when most of your ailments are no longer curable and you just have to learn to live with them.

It may be sweet to do nothing, as the saying goes, but after a while it becomes boring.

Men of great intelligence can sometimes be great fools.

We should train our minds as we train our bodies, but it's much harder.

One can enjoy life without being an expert in anything.

Nationalism is just another form of tribalism, and too often that's the case with religion as well.

Rhetoric, alas, is more powerful than reason.

Places that are the height of the exotic to us are banal to those who live there.

We are all narcissists one way or another

Ingénues are a thing of the past.

You know you're old when, gathering with others your age, you invariably discuss your illnesses.

It's hard for us to imagine that our grandparents weren't always old.

The difference between the French and the English is that the French hyphenate their first names, the English their last.

No other animal is as destructive as man.

We're doing our best to become an endangered species.

Confusion can be good. It opens up the mind.

It's our inner space that most needs exploring.

Mythology is replete with heroes. History offers few whose heroism was unalloyed.

If we try hard enough to convince ourselves that the naked are clothed, we'll end up believing it.

Fishing is a sport that tests the intelligence of man against that of fish.

A weed doesn't think of itself as noxious.

One way of becoming wise is to make lots of mistakes.

The trouble with the military is that they have an overriding interest in winning that conflicts with their ability to see the wisdom of withdrawal.

We shouldn't trust the military when they assure us they can win a war any more than we should have trusted tobacco executives when they told us that cigarettes didn't cause cancer.

If a group of people try hard enough to convince themselves and each other of an absurdity, they'll usually end up believing it. This is what's known as group think, or ideology, or religion.

It might be a better world if adults skipped.

We put too much faith in the integrity of the written word.

L'enfer, c'est nous.

Women are superior to men. They laugh at themselves more readily.

It's foolish to go around the world trying to find yourself. Wherever you are, you're there.

Today's new thing is tomorrow's history.

We are what we read.

It's liberating to feel free to tell embarrassing truths about oneself.

The true hero is he who avoids violence.

Those things we wish to be so we tend to believe to be so.

If you leave things in the same place long enough, they become invisible.

The trouble with running on automatic pilot is that it isn't necessarily programmed to take you where you want to go.

The human race is a Greek tragedy waiting to happen.

We constantly strive for a transcendence that doesn't exist.

The first sign of aging is disliking snow.

We're often not satisfied for things to be as they are. We want them to be more significant.

Civilization is a process of transcending instinct.

Colonels kick ass. Babies kick air.

The human need to make sense of everything leads to much nonsense.

Humans are animals that think they're not animals.

Empathy is the root of all virtue.

We remember best the things we'd most like to forget.

Children learn by mimicking without questioning whether what they mimic is right or wrong. Unfortunately, many continue to do this as adults.

The marathon is an ego trip.

Being smart doesn't protect us from self-deception. In fact, it may make us more adept at it.

Humor is one of the best weapons.

The trouble with theory is that it often blinds us to reality.

Ishtar, also known as Astarte, was the goddess of love and war. The ancients knew things about human relationships from which psychologists could learn.

If Narcissus had had a camera, he would have spent his days taking selfies.

Smartness isn't the same thing as intelligence. Smartness is mental ability. Intelligence is what you do with your smartness.

Intelligence doesn't assure rationality.

Snobbery is irrational. It's based on pedigree, celebrity and manners rather than contribution or accomplishment.

Rooting for a team is another kind of tribalism.

Everybody should spend a few minutes a day in bumper cars. Road rage would become passé.

The road of life is pitted with rabbit holes.

Youth is fond of newness.

We find capriciousness in a young woman charming. When she gets older it's another story.

Love of country is often no more than self-love. We consider ourselves worthy because we think our country is.

Cultivation of empathy is a more effective basis for ethical behavior than instilling fear of punishment, here or in the hereafter. We're too easily convinced that punishment isn't likely or even (as among Islamist terrorists or ideological autocrats and their followers) that acts harmful to others are virtuous. On the other hand, empathy is an instinct that, once activated, can't be rationalized away.

What is subject to endless growth? Cancer and the human race.

Man is an apex predator.

Death isn't the worst thing that can happen to you.

It makes one happy to make somebody else happy.

We labor under the illusion that insults win arguments.

Anger is contagious.

People who are interested are interesting.

Only the old have the wisdom to enjoy all the blessings of youth.

Marx's notion that, when workers take charge, utopia will follow, though an understandable product of its time, was, like all utopias, an illusion. The enemy isn't capitalism. It's human nature.

Philosophy

One Tycho Brahe or William Harvey is worth three Aristotles or five Platos.

The question, 'What is the sound of one hand clapping?', rather than a profound paradox, is an example of human gullibility.

Philosophy is a mental rope trick. One's conclusions depend on one's assumptions.

If we don't take sinners seriously as moral philosophers, who's left?

Philosophy is a form of thought that attempts to know by reason that which is a matter of opinion or is only knowable empirically and for which there's no empirical evidence.

Profundity

We confound the obscure with the profound.

Many can't distinguish pretense from profundity; their instinct when faced with something they don't understand is to ascribe deep significance to it.

Profundity should bring us closer to truth. Most of what passes for profound moves in the opposite direction.

Profundity isn't so much the revelation of difficult to discern truths as the setting aside of deeply rooted notions.

There are no deeper meanings, only feelings.

Ambiguity isn't profound. It's just ambiguous.

The line between the profound and the sententious is anything but clear.

The trouble with theory is that it often blinds us to reality.

Beware of big ideas.

Sometimes things can be so subtle they're imperceptible.

Politics

Just say no? What kind of philosophy of life is that?

Conservatism is the politics of self-interest.

The greatest leaders are those who lead people to restrain their self-interest and emotions.

For a conservative, progress means going back to earlier times.

Plato overlooked an important point. An aristocracy of intellect can be as self-interested and tyrannical as one of birth, money or priesthood.

Why should the integrity of nation states be sacrosanct?

When an allegation is characterized as absolutely ridiculous, you can be pretty sure it's true.

Outrageous remarks, it seems, are always taken out of context.

The most important measure of civilization is compassion, not technology, culture, sophisticated institutions, power or the gross national product.

Extremism isn't a matter of how far one is from the prevailing middle but of how far one is from a defensible position.

In greed we trust.

They speak of government of laws, not of men. But who makes the laws? And who interprets them?

We've progressed. Patriotism is no longer the last refuge of scoundrels. It's the first.

The Gestapo were all patriots.

Liberté, Égalité, Sororité.

Knowledge and intelligence, however great, are no guaranty of objectivity or impartiality.

A bird in the hand is worth any number of Bushes.

The belief in a perfect society is one of the most destructive ideas concocted by mankind.

Advice to future Republican administrations: put the supply of combat forces out for competitive bidding; privatize Congress; outsource the Presidency.

Conservatism is the belief that that good old-time religion should prevail, and that the haves should get to keep all they can lay their hands on.

Conservatism: an unholy alliance of religion and money.

We've gone through the me generation; we're now into the me century.

Liberal means tolerant and generous. Are these bad things?

Unfortunately, when it comes to politics, you can fool too many of the people too much of the time.

Bush was caught between Iraq and a hard place.

Is there such a thing as intellectually honest conservatives? Perhaps, but if so, you can count them on the fingers of less than one hand.

A right winger is someone who loves Jesus but favors the death penalty, preemptive war and punishing poor Central Americans for trying to make a decent living.

Conservatives see no contradiction in being pro-life on the one hand and against gun control, in favor of the death penalty, indifferent or hostile to universal health care and war hawks on the other.

It's not so sweet to die for one's country in a pointless war, and most wars are pointless.

Executive privilege is what a President invokes when he or someone who has worked closely with him is lying.

Destiny is never manifest.

'Fiscal conservatives' are those who despise altruism, except where it saves them from having to pay taxes.

The best conservatives are those who are cautious about change, prefer prudence to audacity and evolution to revolution, are wary of excessive government and are intellectually honest, but that's a very rare breed.

How civilized a country is can be measured by its willingness to give autonomy or independence to ethnic enclaves.

The Chinese are right. Before their conquest of Tibet it was dominated by aristocrats and monks who owned the land and treated peasant farmers like serfs. Now Tibet is dominated by the Chinese government, which owns the land and treats all Tibetans like serfs.

It's time to put the hens in charge of the foxes' dens.

Be careful about voting for the presidential candidate you'd rather have a beer with. You might end up with suds in the White House.

Sovereignty: the right of nations to abuse their citizens, and claimed citizens, without outside interference.

Conservatism is the politics of the tribe.

A spin doctor is just another kind of quack.

Beware of those who wave the flag. They're usually waving it for some irrational or self-serving reason.

When our loved ones die in an arguably necessary war, that's a tragedy. When they die in an unnecessary one, it's a crime.

It's too bad the south didn't win the civil war. If it had, we wouldn't be burdened with Texas.

Compassionate conservatism is an oxymoron.

Conservatives' belief in trickledown isn't much different from children's belief in Santa Claus.

The trouble with U.S. liberals is that they tend just to talk to each other while the conservatives talk to the voters.

Compassionate conservatism means compassion for one's fellow conservatives and not much for anybody else.

Forget about Jesus. What would Ronald Reagan do?

There's a danger in leadership of becoming wedded to its formula for success while the world moves on.

Conservatives are for comfort for the comfortable. The rest is rationalization.

Those who win power by force tend to rule by force. This is the fate of revolutions.

Conservative, in politics, has become a euphemism for mean-spirited.

Conservatives don't really object to big government. They just object to having to help pay for it.

Conservative politics is a meeting of the minds between those interested in preserving tradition and those interested in preserving their wealth.

Libertarianism would free us from government restrictions, or oppression if you will, and free us to oppress others or be oppressed by them.

A conservative is one who wants to impose his beliefs on and preserve his assets and privileges at the expense of others.

There aren't arms races. There's only been one, and it started when men first picked up sticks and stones to batter then impale one another. Since then there's been a constant escalation in technology and cost so that we devote more and more of our gross national products to the means of killing one another.

In politics, while some want to do what's right, other's want merely to rationalize their self-interest.

There are those who have honest differences on public policy based on what they think the results are likely to be, and there are those, usually at the political extremes, who use sophistry, appeal to emotion, distortion and even outright lies to support their beliefs.

What distinguishes America's great leaders is that they were great for their goodness, not for their aptitude as conquerors.

Those who are against a war are usually right.

If you cling to the center of the road, you're likely to get run over.

If fascism ever comes to America, it'll start in Texas.

Conservatism is inevitably flawed by its alliance with privilege.

According to contemporary Republicans, conservation isn't conservative.

Those are most warlike who have never fought and think they never will.

Never trust conspiracy theorists. Their distrust of others is a projection of their own untrustworthiness.

If you want to find the anti-Christ, you don't need to look any farther than the fundamentalists, the Tea Party, Texas and the NRA.

Constitutional originalism is the American version of Sharia.

Private enterprise and free markets can't be trusted to do the right thing any more than government. What's needed with the former, as with the latter, is checks and balances.

Beware of those who preach national glory.

The problem in our country isn't big government. It's big money.

American civilization won't be destroyed by barbarian invaders but by ideologues quoting the Constitution.

A conservative is someone who doesn't change his or her beliefs even when those beliefs are contradicted by evidence.

The magic of the market is supposed to be good. Whether capitalism is good or bad depends on who's using the term.

Contemporary conservatism is an amalgam of a number of virtues; self-interest, greed, callousness, mean spiritedness, tribalism, nationalism, xenophobia, jingoism, punitiveness, vindictiveness, a belief in patriarchy, theocratic tendencies, superstition and an aversion to change.

'Intellectually honest conservative' has become an oxymoron.

Most academics are liberal because most of those who seek the truth are, while the vast majority of conservatives seek not truth but justification for their preconceptions.

Conservatives are those who are most concerned about maintaining their own benefits and privileges and/or enforcing religious strictures. Liberals are those who are most concerned about the needs of others.

Freedom Caucus is a euphemism for the law of the jungle.

Libertarianism is seductive in its simplicity, but in the end it's simplistic.

Patriotism that places the interests of one nation over fairness and compassion for all isn't a virtue but an evil.

The free market undermines itself with too much freedom.

Patriotism too easily becomes chauvinism.

Most conservatives want to preserve tradition no matter how unjust or unjustifiable it may be.

Jesus was a socialist.

We argue over whether the American dream is alive or dead, but let us not forget that a dream is not reality.

The influence of women on public policy is too important for them to just 'stay at home and have children'.

We don't have a problem of the tyranny of the majority in America. We have a problem of the tyranny of a minority.

The danger of Sharia in America doesn't come from Islam. It comes from home-grown evangelicals.

Free market fundamentalism isn't the solution. It's the problem.

A conservative is one who believes that morning-after contraception is murder but exposing your fellow humans to the COVID virus by refusing to wear a mask is your constitutional right.

Economics

Economists want to quantify everything. How do you quantify *joie de vivre*, natural beauty, love?

Economic growth is a tiger from which we fear to dismount.

If there were a choice between economic growth and a decent life for all, which would be the better choice?

All but a very few economists are devotees of the cult of growth.

The world would be a better place if we were less concerned about more and more about better.

What's more important, that our economy grow by one, two or three percent *ad infinitum* or that everybody have decent health care, education, housing and employment?

Economic growth is wonderful, but along with the goods it brings us a lot of garbage, junk food and last year's fashions, the things we excitedly acquired and soon never looked at again.

Economics should be not about more, always more, but about meeting the basic needs of all. Beyond that we would be better served by pursuing happiness through non-material means rather than through the endless acquisition of things.

Money is like a gas. It tends to float up rather than trickle down.

The elimination of poverty is more important than the creation of wealth. Wealth should be seen as first and foremost a means for ending poverty.

It's the economy that counts. Don't worry about people.

Where does the Bible say that economic growth is the greatest good?

With its top-heavy income distribution, America is coming more and more to resemble a dystopian fantasy.

The trouble with 'the invisible hand' is that you don't know what it's up to when you can't see it.

Life is like a game of cards. It depends to a considerable extent on the hand you're dealt.

Justice

We're each determined never to yield to force, yet we always expect others to do so.

Violence tends to escalate, whether perpetrated by those outside the law, or those within it.

Violence is rarely the solution.

The latest euphemism for prison is correctional facility. Criminalization facility would be more apt.

Someone in possession of a gram of crack cocaine is a felon. Someone who brings great harm, even death, to thousands through the sale of a legal product is a pillar of society.

We've just completed a 30 years' war on drugs and are going for 100.

In divorce and the war on drugs we must take care that victory doesn't do as much harm to the victors as to the vanquished.

What if there were no heaven or hell and no redemption and after we died we spent all eternity experiencing again and again the good we have done others but also the harm and the results of our failures to do good?

Vengeance may be the Lord's, but we have victim's rights.

Vengeance is out of fashion. It's been replaced by closure.

Think about how to get what you want, not how to punish the person standing in the way of your getting it.

If you can't make it better, let it go. Revenge costs time and energy that simply add to the damage

Criminal justice is an oxymoron for the very rich and the very poor.

The legal profession is more about money than justice.

The Supreme Court should strive to avoid the initiation of constitutional amendments which can have unforeseen consequences much greater than any judicial interpretation and are much harder to reverse. To achieve this purpose, the Court must not get too far behind or ahead of public opinion.

Religion

I don't need to be reborn. I got it right the first time.

God seems to be on the side of the biggest bucks.

The Bible is another of those Rorschach tests. All see what they fancy in it.

'Theology' is an oxymoron.

Apocalypse is always tomorrow.

Where would the world be without heresy?

One man's piety is another's blasphemy.

Morality has nothing to do with sex and everything to do with how you treat your fellow man.

Do you suppose that God cares more about property rights than he does about the well-being of all his creatures?

There are those who are proud of their humility.

If you want to know the meaning of life, look in a dictionary.

The great mystery of religion is that anyone can believe the doctrines propagated in its name.

The Crusaders may have claimed more victims than the Huns.

The purpose of life is life.

We have a new version of the golden rule; do unto others whatever will do most for you.

Stoicism, Buddhist detachment, piety and altruism are all ways of escaping painful or unsettling feelings.

Faith without reason is not a social good.

Let's not forget that faith is by definition irrational.

Revealed truth is incompatible with sound social policy.

If we devoted more attention to ethics and less to religious dogma, the world would be a better place.

Of the four forms of utopianism that flourished in the 20th century, fundamentalism, communism, fascism and anarchism only fundamentalism continues to thrive in this the 21st.

Does God have a penis? If so, why?

We don't need the devil to account for evil. Human nature is explanation enough.

The devil is a convenient excuse for our own worst instincts.

Who is the source of punitive religion, God or the devil?

What kind of god would care how you worshiped him, or even whether you did?

It's curious that those who still believe lust is a sin more often than not believe that greed no longer is.

Sinners are drawn to Catholicism. It's hospitable to sin.

Worship of a deity is the original cult of personality.

There isn't one antichrist but many and they aren't godlike demons but ordinary folk who negate Christ's message of compassion while professing their love of him.

You can't love Jesus and hate your fellow man.

When it comes to salvation, only you can save yourself; no one else can save you.

Theology is the rationalization of the irrational.

The most discriminated against minority in America is atheists.

If one god is better than two or more, surely no god is best of all.

Don't put your trust in leaders who profess to believe in the literal truth of scripture. These are men who don't want to be troubled by evidence.

Add priests to a collection of myths and superstitions and you get a religion.

The world would be a better place if men spent more time buggering each other and less shooting, bombing, bashing and skewering.

If you profess your love of Jesus enough, you can get away with just about anything.

The conviction that religious beliefs other than one's own are false leads to all sorts of strife and mistreatment of one's fellow humans.

Fundamentalists may say that God is love, but actually they believe He is hate.

The first principle of ethics: permit no real harm in the name of theological harm.

Some engage in jihads, others conduct crusades. Let us all instead wage peace.

The religious right is right. Evolution is supposed to make us better adapted, but look what's happening to the American mind.

The world took a big step backward when Christianity and then Islam took to the idea of divinely dictated scripture.

The believers have turned reverence for (human) life into a form of idolatry.

When we win or have good fortune, we praise God. Why is it we never blame Him when we don't?

Intelligent design is the philosophy of the planned economy.

Saintliness isn't a matter of piety or miracles. It's a matter of compassion, conviction and courage.

Religion has been good for architecture.

Much harm has been done in the name of that which is deemed sacred.

Would Jesus have voted for George W. Bush? Or Donald Trump?

It's clear that man isn't descended from the monkey. No monkey is capable of the evils wrought by men.

Beware the undead and the born again.

People aren't good or bad so much because of what they believe as because of what they feel.

There's an awful lot that's unchristian about Christianity.

Let us pray for the Roman Catholics. May the Lord Our God enlighten their hearts so that they may acknowledge that the pope is anything but infallible.

Enlightenment isn't a total transformation. It's a piecemeal, imperfect and never complete process.

The Bible says that God slew the first born of the Egyptians to make them let the Israelites go. The authors of the good book apparently considered terrorism a legitimate tool of conflict.

I can't imagine anything more boring than nirvana.

When we find there's no rational answer, we look to mysticism to provide one.

I haven't seen any evidence that the meek will inherit the earth. Maybe the cockroaches.

The only eternal truth is that there are no eternal truths.

The devil is anything but an atheist.

Religion is too often hijacked by the violent.

The real miracle of religion is the things people believe in its name.

Jesus's message wasn't 'Love me'. It was 'Love your fellow man'.

America isn't a Christian nation. It's a Protestant, Catholic, Jewish, Muslim, Buddhist, Hindu, Mormon, Sikh, Rastafarian, Voodoo, Bahai, Wiccan, atheist nation.

The first multinational was the Catholic Church, and it still places corporate interests before public.

You don't need a guru to find peace. You can find it within yourself.

If you want to know the truth about a religion, don't ask anyone who considers it the truth.

One man's revelation is another's delusion.

In most cases, irreverence is more justifiable than reverence.

Don't look to theologians for truth. They're an interest group.

The secret of sacred mysteries is that there is no secret.

I consider religion a buffet from which I pick the good dishes and leave aside the dog meat and entrails.

What is the meaning of life is a meaningless question.

Morality doesn't interest me. I'm concerned about ethics.

C.S. Lewis depicted God as a lion. The lion, of course, is a predator.

The most important thing religion brings to society and the one most often lacking in the way religions are practiced, is compassion. It's interesting that the ten commandments have nothing to say about it.

If the story of Adam and Eve is true, we are all products of incest.

When a religion becomes reasonable it loses believers.

What if Lucifer was a whistle blower?

The meaning of life is life.

Theology isn't a search for truth. It's a search for justification.

If there is a God, He must be rolling His eyes.

Who am I to tell people what to do with their genitals?

Many of those who profess their Christianity most vociferously, when it comes to compassion, central to Jesus's message, are Chinos, Christians in name only.

If the fundamentalists had their way, America would look like the Islamic Republic of Iran.

The only difference between a cult and a religion is the number of people who believe in it and for how long.

Anyone who says they know what God thinks is either delusional or a fraud.

A religion arises when a large number of people believe in a series of implausible and unverifiable events for a long enough period of time.

Efforts to impose Christian orthodoxy—school prayer, the teaching of intelligent design, vouchers for attendance at religious schools, anti-contraception policies, etcetera—are a far greater threat to our society than sharia.

Why would God have had to conceive a son and sacrifice him to free mankind from original sin? If omnipotent, couldn't he have just done it directly?

If Jesus and God are one, as the doctrine of the holy trinity holds, Jesus didn't need to suffer on the cross. He could have simply decided not to. In fact, for all we know, he did.

To think God cares what you eat or what sort of sexual practices you engage in is to view the Almighty is some sort of pettifogging legal clerk.

Religiosity is most often proportionate to lack of education.

The most important value religion can offer is compassion.

Judge people not by what they profess to believe but by what they do.

Homosexuality is no more unnatural than chastity, maybe even less so.

If you spend too much time worrying about the next life, you may lose the chance to enjoy the only one you've got.

Virtue isn't a matter of what you do for yourself but of what you do for others.

The pious are often of the opinion that those who don't share their brand of piety deserve extreme punishment or at least deprivation of their rights.

The Bible and related stories are, of course, victor's history. Lucifer, had he had the opportunity, might have offered a different account.

It's significant that sacred is an anagram for scared.

We think that God favors humans over all his other creations. Why would he favor such a destructive creature?

Morality has little to do with ethics.

Folly

Man's stupidity is almost equaled by his intelligence.

For all our mastery of technology, we're still prey to follies as flagrant as those of any earlier age.

Though our understanding of things biological, mechanical and electronic has increased manyfold, our capacity for self-deception hasn't diminished one whit.

While we laugh or rage at others' follies, we view our own as possessing the greatest dignity and worth.

Each age is convinced that its follies represent the highest level of human achievement.

Being a genius doesn't prevent one from having foolish ideas.

Much of what most people believe is nonsense.

Fashion

People not only don't mention that the emperor wears no clothes, they've convinced themselves that it's not the case, and what's more think it high fashion.

There are many emperors and many who are blind to their nakedness.

We have trouble remembering that form is not substance.

What's fashionable today is passé tomorrow.

Fashion makes fools of us all.

Those who live by fashion die by the same.

Today's cutting edge is tomorrow's old guard.

We live in an age of irony, one of retreat from life.

We adopt irony because we think it puts us above our fellows, but it also makes us less alive.

Irony is a post-modern form of egocentricity.

Ars gratia vanitatis.

The good word 'gay' has been sequestered. It can no longer be used to mean lighthearted. We should worry about words the way we worry about endangered species.

The good thing about the rapid pace of change in our times is that few fads last very long.

Let us kick off the shackles of fashion.

Today's blue chip is tomorrow's recyclable trash.

Materialism

We think we're what we accumulate.

Man does not live by bread alone. He also lives by iPods, camera cell phones, Xboxes, LCD HD TVs, SUVs, McMansions and Cancun vacations.

Collecting is a poor substitute for creativity.

Diamonds are for people without imagination.

We're always chasing after more, but there's always more to be had.

Enough is never enough.

Ars gratia commercii.

Let's not forget that greed is a sin.

We have so many possessions in our affluent society that they get lost in the crowd. We often can't find them when we want them or don't even know we have them.

Our lives are consumed by conveniences.

In a consumer society, invention is the mother of necessity.

There are many activities in life that are more fulfilling than trying to get the best price.

Today the money changers are no longer just in the temple. They're its priests.

Too many of us have deep pockets and shallow values.

The more extravagant the wedding, the shorter the marriage.

The term 'bull market' is apt in more ways than one.

We're obsessed with getting more, more of everything. We might be better off if we devoted our attention instead on how to make do with less.

The Arts

Innovation in the arts has become hackneyed.

We make up for the rejection of the impressionists by accepting anything as good art as long as it's new.

War has been good for literature.

If your name is Stein, don't name your daughter Phyllis.

In art, character and observation are more important than story. In entertainment, it's the other way around.

Whether a story is good or not isn't a matter of where it goes but how it gets there.

A thing of beauty is a joy until you get used to it.

Conceptual art: too much concept, too little art.

The avant-garde is no longer the vanguard. It's a lost detachment of foot soldiers milling around in a cul-de-sac.

When everything is avant-garde, nothing is avant-garde.

Once an artist demonstrates his brilliance, we see brilliance in whatever he does however nonsensical.

Literature these days suffers from excessive self-consciousness.

Oppression is the mother of literary invention.

If you want something new in literature, you don't need to resort to stylistic novelty, nonsense or conundrums. Each and every one of us is different in experience and worldview.

We're so obsessed with innovation and originality that we accept any sort of nonsense as long as it's different from our usual way of saying things.

Writers who have been workshopped have been sawn, assembled, planed, sanded and lacquered. Is that what we want in our writers?

In the end, fashion is the enemy of art.

Intellectualization is good for analysis but not for art. The 20th Century was an era of intellectualization of the arts.

Art that tries to create art most often fails. Art does better when it strives to create reality.

The artful slides all too easily into the arty.

The hallmark of serious fiction is perspicacious observation of how people behave and what they think and feel.

All good literature is at bottom realism.

In the attempt to become more and more significant, the arts are becoming less and less meaningful.

French culture is deathly ill, of too much French culture.

The arts have become avatars of the fashion industry.

The modernist revolution is no longer a revolution. It's the establishment.

Post-modern is more modern than post.

Can't one remember without alluding to Proust?

Bad wars make good movies.

When an artistic fashion is appreciated by few but the cognoscenti, it's either revolutionary or moribund, usually the latter.

There's something oxymoronic about an academic degree in creative writing.

The world is full of well-written books that don't interest me.

The visual arts have descended to the level of the pet rock.

Sooner or later the cutting edge becomes dull.

Most critics are parasites. They're supposed to illuminate culture but more often simply exploit it.

Critics' main fans are other critics.

Critics of the arts are prey to the delusion that what they like is good and what they don't like is bad.

Originality isn't everything, though many artists seem to think it is.

Modernism is given to allusions, or is it illusions?

Opera: mediocre drama accompanied by sometimes glorious but mostly ho-hum music interspersed with recitative, a singsong form of dialogue which is the musical and dramatic equivalent of plastic wood.

What counts most in the arts these days is self-promotion. We're still in the Warhol age.

Newer isn't necessarily better.

The trouble with editing your own work is that you tend to see what you meant to say rather than what you actually said.

They talk about the banality of evil. What about the evil of banality?

Contemporary rock bands are the musical equivalent of professional wrestling.

Novelty in the arts has gotten old.

There are too many people writing and not enough doing.

Innovation for innovation's sake is as sterile as tradition for tradition's sake.

Intellectualization is the death of art.

Post-modernism is modernism run amok.

Writers used to write about heroes. Now they think they're the heroes.

In the arts everybody wants to be in the vanguard, which means that the vanguard quickly becomes indistinguishable from the rear guard.

Among intellectuals, those who write about deeds are seen as greater heroes than those who perform them.

Poetry

Poetry is the art of the implied.

Poetry is as much about what isn't said as what is.

A poet has to learn to let readers draw the inference rather than drawing it for them.

The poet's role is to reveal things others aren't aware they're seeing.

Poetry in its more esoteric forms is like philosophy and religion. It makes much out of nothing.

Poetry today is in the oracular tradition; the more obscure it is, the more significant it's seen to be.

We consider some poetry we can't understand good or even great not despite our inability to understand it but <u>because</u> we can't understand it.

Poetry is a religion of intellectuals, and would-be intellectuals.

Poetry critics and professors love the cryptic. It gives them something to interpret.

I don't want to have to decipher poetry. I just want to experience it.

Today everybody is a poet's poet. The trouble is that nobody reads them except each other.

There's an arms race among contemporary poets to see who can be the most arcane and solipsistic.

Many contemporary poets think they live in a gated community. Actually, they live in a ghetto, and have locked themselves in.

It's ironic that T.S. Eliot, one of the high priests of modernism, rejected the modern world.

Poetry is a narcissistic business.

In poetry it's difficult to draw a line between substance and style.

The problem with contemporary poetry is that it's become and academic discipline, and fallen down the same hole as sociology and lit crit.

Writing poetry is so popular because it's the only form of writing in which you're not likely to be widely criticized for incomprehensibility.

Some poets hear music in their heads. In others' you hear the grinding of gears.

Why is it that many people think happiness a less suitable subject for poetry than depression?

Poetry is very much an expression of personality.

It isn't the form that makes a poem. It's the feeling.

Beware the poetry-academic complex.

Poetic language isn't so much a matter of precision as connotation.

Intellectualization will be the undoing of postmodern poetry, as sentimentality was of romanticism.

Contemporary poetry has gone down the intellectualized path of serial music, the *nouvel roman* and 20th century art fads. It will recede down the path of obscurity with them too.

If poetry that can mean something different to every reader is good, isn't the ultimate poem a blank sheet of paper?

We think that a poem we have to interpret is more profound than one whose meaning is evident.

Contemporary poetry seldom delights. Reading it is more often a form of forced labor.

Discovering a new poet is like coming upon a land you didn't know existed.

Poetry is being done in by inbreeding.

As poetry becomes less and less relevant, its practitioners and camp followers develop an increasingly inflated notion of its importance.

In striving to be original, poets today have strayed farther and farther from the communicative and apt.

Ultimately what we like or dislike about a poet is his or her worldview.

Exaggeration is one of the most common faults of bad poetry.

Contemporary poetry, like serial music, has alienated its audience. It represents the triumph of theory over experience.

Every reader reading the same poem reads a different one.

In poetry it's the difference between synonyms that counts.

The essence of poetry is feeling. All else is ornamentation.

The best thing that could happen to contemporary poetry would be for universities to do away with all poetry courses.

Mediocre poets like the fashion for obscurity in contemporary poetry. It obscures their mediocrity.

Ultimately what a poem has to say is more important than how it says it.

Poetry that dedicates itself to evoking confusion and uncertainty has essentially only one theme, confusion and uncertainty.

You could write splendid poetry and, if you didn't win the critical attention lottery, it might disappear without a trace and be unknown to future generations.

Contemporary poets try so hard to be different that they mostly end up sounding the same.

When one sculpts a figure in wood or stone, one doesn't shape it, one chisels or carves away the material that conceals it. So it is with the editing of a poem.

Language poetry is a cultural dead end, like *les precieuses ridicules* or 19th century salon painting.

'The Red Wheelbarrow' is a celebrity poem. It's famous because it's famous.

Don't look to poets for eternal truths. They're not philosophers. They're rhetoricians.

Poetry that tries to be philosophy often ends up being good as neither.

Poetry journals, of which there are so many, are published not so much for the benefit of poets, much less readers, as to feed the self-importance of their publishers.

There's so much poetry being written these days that, if it were thrown away all in the same place, it would create a landfill of epic proportions.

Finding a poem one likes is like panning for gold. One has to sift through a lot of mud and grit to turn up a bit of the shiny stuff.

The impact of some poems is dulled by their artistry.

The Emperor of Ice-Cream wears no clothes.

Most poetry today is not heartfelt, but headfelt, which, of course, is an oxymoron, or a headache.

Oppression is a wonderful stimulus to the arts. Contemporary American poetry could use some of it.

There are important similarities between poetry and religion. Both involve incantation, mystification and reverence.

Yeats thought the Byzantium of 1000 AD a high point of civilization. That tells you more about Yeats than about Byzantium.

Nonsense verse often makes more sense than that which is seen by the poetry authorities as deeply serious.

Before you write a poem ask yourself would this be interesting if it weren't a poem? If the answer is no, it won't be interesting just because you cast it in poetic form.

Poets have long struggled for precision and evocativeness in their language. Post-modern poets strive for ambiguity and puzzling disconnection between words and images, creating riddles with multiple possible solutions.

I don't belong to a school of poets. I belong to myself.

The power of poetry is in feeling, not metaphysics.

Postmodern poetry has gone on far too long. It's become innovation for innovation's sake.

Poetry is that which evokes the ineffable.

Some poetry is magical, or at least a feat of prestidigitation, but much of it is three card monte.

In poetry, music is as important as meaning.

One man's allusion is another's obscurantism.

Calculation is no substitute for inspiration. Contemporary poetry is 90% calculation.

Advice

Love people for what they are, not for what you'd like them to be.

Beware of Greeks bearing myths.

Concern yourself with what you can do, not what you can't.

Resist thinking of an argument as a competition you have to win.

Marry a woman who likes your jokes.

If you speak in code, don't be surprised if you're misunderstood.

Never patronize a restaurant advertising fine food, and never trust anyone who says trust me.

Shake your fist in dance, not in anger.

Indignation is good for you. It clears the sinuses.

When somebody asks you if you'd like some feedback, say, 'No thanks'. And, if you want to be really polite, you can add after a moment, 'Thank you for not sharing that with me'.

Beware of wisdom. It can make you pompous.

Distrust gurus.

The most important thing to know is the limits of one's knowledge.

Being clear about the question is more important than having a plausible but unsubstantiated answer.

Ignorance is bliss, until it turns around and bites you.

Remembering the rules doesn't do much good unless you understand the reasons behind them.

Know yourself or fool yourself.

Never trust a man who has no sense of humor.

Be your own guru.

Etcetera

Patriotism, piety and chastity are all much overrated virtues.

Force is less often the solution than we're inclined to think.

Icarus wouldn't have made a very good rocket scientist.

Bombs are careless in their choice of targets.

Today Scrooge would be a libertarian.

Civilization is too often built on the backs of ordinary men.

The grass is often greener on the other side of the street because it's been painted.

Eden is not a place but a state of mind.

Most adventures are in the mind.

We lavish subsidies on the having of children as if the world were insufficiently populated.

Things are universal in their particularity.

Innovations are seldom as consequential as advocates fancy or doubters fear.

Concern for humankind trumps patriotism any time.

My primary allegiances are to family, friends and the human race. All others are secondary.

While some prophecies are self-fulfilling, others are self-defeating.

'Pretentious' is a pretentious word.

We used to have voices in the wilderness. Now we have voices in cyberspace.

We do not live by efficiency alone.

You may not be able to make a silk purse out of a sow's ear, but you can make something that looks an awful lot like one.

Dessert can never be too soon.

There is no demonstrable right or wrong. There are merely altruism and egoism, compassion and indifference, consistency and inconsistency, self-awareness and self-deception.

One's workload expands to exceed the time available for it.

Talking with some people isn't dialogue; it's an interrupted monologue.

Our world is like a dog chasing its tail, the crazy calling the crazy crazy.

Not only are there emperors who have no clothes, most of them aren't even emperors.

You can fool too many of the people too much of the time.

They say that time is money, but you can make money. You can't make time.

Tomorrow may not be another day.

Some bombs are smarter than others, but they're all dumb.

It's dirt poor or filthy rich. Only the middle class is clean.

Compassion and generosity are by far the most important virtues.

The most dangerously insane are those who by clinical criteria are sane, the demagogues, the jingoists, the racists, the conspiracy theorists, the true believers.

As for capitalism I say, don't kill the goose that lays the golden eggs. Just don't let it run wild in the barnyard.

I'm no longer into road rage. Customer service rage has left it in the dust.

Death is a funny fellow, all dressed up like the anti-hero of a Hollywood horror flick.

There are enough real puzzles in the world that no one should feel the need to struggle with contrived ones.

There's a fine line between logic and sophistry.

'We have zero tolerance' means we used to tolerate it, but we got caught.

If Sisyphus were alive today, he wouldn't be pushing a rock up a hill. It would be a lawn mower.

Experience can blind us to what's happening now.
This is the eternal weakness of military strategizing.

A cow may be sacred, but it's still a cow.

Yoga is a path to enlightenment through contortionism.

There is no limit to the number of territories one can find, journeying inward.

I grew up in a nuclear family and raised my children in one. In between there was the threat of nuclear war. Now that's all changed. It's gone nucular.

Insomnia is my constant companion. It goes to bed with me like a spouse and is there when I awake.

Our planet, enjoy it while you still can.

The difference between the old world and the new is that here in the new world we have all night grocery stores, but we don't have nightingales.

You don't need to travel far to find the unfamiliar. You just need to dig a little deeper where you are.

Reinventing the wheel isn't a bad idea. You sometimes come up with a better wheel.

It doesn't matter much where I live geographically. Basically, I live in my mind.

Genius isn't just a matter of seeing things others don't see. It's also a matter of what you do with your insights.

Edison said that genius is 1% inspiration, 99% perspiration. His work ethic was commendable, but without the 1% the 99% is worth next to nothing.

Birth is our first traumatic experience.

We produce too many lawyers and financiers in America and too few engineers.

Many books could be reduced to articles without significant loss.

We tell people what time to come to dinner. Too bad it isn't the custom to tell them also what time to leave.

The worst thing about sex isn't sexually transmitted diseases or unwanted pregnancies but the overpopulation it creates.

If a baker's dozen is 13, a financier's is 9. The missing quarter is the financier's fee.

Soldiering is considered an honorable profession, but is it a civilized one? Soldiers are honored as much for humiliating and killing our enemies as for defending us.

The answer to lies or insults isn't suppression. That inevitably results in the suppression of truth. The answer to lies or insults is truth.

What to us stinks, to a vulture is gourmet food.

Laughter is one of the best gifts of the gods.

What I want to know is when they are going to make croquet and tiddlywinks Olympic sports.

If you launder dirty money, does that makes it clean lucre?

Paris is a cliché.

Few slopes are slippery.

Dogs are friendly, clumsy clowns. Cats are aloof, lithe and dignified, but killers.

Where there's no winter there's no spring.

There's no such thing as a little email.

Orthodoxy leads to stagnation, or worse.

We only ever know an interpretation, not just of history, but of events we're living through.

Sometimes the whole is less than the sum of the parts.

Just because we admire someone doesn't mean we should approve of them. Think Napoleon.

We should be more concerned about goodness than greatness.

Efforts to create utopias usually result in dystopias.

One picture may be worth a thousand words, but a few words may be worth thousands of pictures.

What is subject to endless growth? Cancer and the human race.

Life is a perpetual motion machine.

'Legal ethics' are a justification for lawyers being unethical on behalf of their clients.

Those who live by publicity shall die by publicity.

It isn't clear that the world wouldn't be a better place if there were no lawyers.

Many a great man ends up shat upon by pigeons.

The past isn't always prologue to the future.

Information technology may be the solution, but it's also very much the problem.

Aphorisms always exaggerate.

It is a truth universally acknowledged that no truth is universally acknowledged.

We all have some magpie within us.

Those who live by the zeitgeist die by the zeitgeist.

In our inadequate response to climate change we're playing Russian roulette with civilization.

Oxymorons:

abstract expressionism

compassionate conservatism

conservative think tank scholar

criminal justice system

customer service

legal ethics

theology.

Finis

www.ingramcontent.com/pod-product-compliance
Lightning Source LLC
Chambersburg PA
CBHW060209050426
42446CB00013B/3027